I0162620

TO LOVE WHILE BLACK IS TO RIOT

To Love While Black Is to Riot
Copyright © 2020 by Whitney Regina Williams
All rights reserved.

This book or parts thereof may not be reproduced in any form,
stored in any retrieval system, or transmitted in any form by
any means—electronic, mechanical, photocopy, recording, or
otherwise—without prior written permission of the publisher,
except as provided by United States of America copyright law.

Warning: The unauthorized reproduction or distribution of a
copyrighted work is illegal. Criminal copyright infringement,
including infringement without monetary gain, is investigated by
the FBI and is punishable by up to five years in federal prison
and a fine of $250,000.

Correspondence may be addressed to
reginawilliamspoetry@gmail.com

Image(s) used under license from depositphotos.com.
Title page illustration: Antonio Navarrette
ISBN 978-0-578-77401-5 (Paperback)
Printed and Bound in the United States of America
First Edition, First Printing

TO

LOVE

WHILE

BLACK

IS

TO

RIOT

REGINA WILLIAMS

a map for the curious

for those who are fighting the good fight

and holding their hearts in their hands.

for my mama. for my grandma. for my dad.

love cannot be destroyed or challenged.

black lives matter.

justice for _____

my love will protect you

from the onslaught of the storm.

when the rain begins to pelt us like bullets,

i will pull myself over you

and i'll face the lightning alone.

my love will protect you

from the onslaught of the storm.

as i walk you to the bus stop,

i won't scold you for jumping into puddles

or spinning around in circles

because the world already sees your gentle carelessness

as a threat.

my love will protect you

from the onslaught of the storm.

i'll cover your eyes with my hands,

so the bodies of men

who look like you on the ten o'clock news

don't taint your innocent vision.

i'll plug your ears

so the cries of their mothers don't flood your heart with fear.

my love will protect you

from the onslaught of the storm.

when we are having adventures on the sidewalk

outside our home,

(you are a knight in shining armor

and i am the loyal sidekick who brings you lemonade

and watches morning cartoons with you)

i won't know how to save the day when you see the

headlights of a patrol car down the road

and you ask me,

"mama, is he gonna shoot us?"

my love will protect you

from the onslaught of the storm.

i will kiss the palms of your hands

and tell you to keep your head held high.

my baby boy,

this world won't cut you down

before i can grow you up.

love letters on old parchment

you are love letters written on old parchment.

you are dipped in ink

and brushed on a surface so delicate

that it can only be preserved by

the passion that comes with aged art.

if i could draw you in

with the words that i write

i'd be the quill and the ink.

i'd take you to far-away places

deep within the confines of our scrolls.

the world has not been kind to you.

your pages are dog-eared.

they are crinkled and folded and abused,

they are curdling like spoiled milk

and your words are smudged.

your instabilities,

your disgraces and flaws,

they are what make you

a work of art.

arrest the cops
who killed breonna taylor

an ode to the one whose hands were used to heal.

whose dreams were soft, selfless, and full of compassion.

who wished to nurse the sick and cure the wounded

like the women before her.

whose fingers laced another's, and whose

palms pressed together as they prayed for a family.

an ode to the one whose heart was used to love.

whose soul was sculpted precisely by God.

each lovely attribute, each empathetic spark,

intermingled through the galaxy that she was,

that her memory continues to be.

an ode to the one whose mind was used to defy all odds.

whose brilliance radiated with a pen and paper,

a cap and gown, a vision of a higher degree.

whose excellence pushed her to new limits,

new branches to climb, new roads to journey,

7

new destinations to reach.

an ode to the one whose life was stolen
at tender twenty-six.
to the chaos that will ensue
until justice is served.

to the peace that is forever disrupted.
to the marches, to the righteous anger,
to the love we must show to her memory.
an ode to breonna.
her boldness, her brilliance, her blackness.

June 5, 1993 - March 13, 2020

daylight

i would trade

one hundred chatty evenings,

one thousand giggly afternoons,

for one quiet morning

with you.

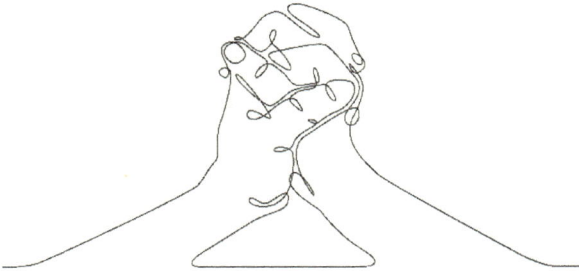

sleeping isn't a crime

beautiful girl with braids down the side of her face,

with joy in her eyes that said "hello world,

i am here, and i am blessed to be here".

with kindness overflowing in her heart like a waterfall,

crashing and showering those around her.

stolen from this world with cruelty

by cowardly men in blue.

small girl of seven years,

resting next to Grandmother, resting under

blankets soft enough to protect her from the

monsters under the bed

but not the monsters outside of her home.

forty minutes past midnight

the devil himself slithered into her home

with their cameras on and rolling,

determined with their intention to make a compelling story

for television.

bullets hidden under their sleeves like magicians,

they tossed in their grenades and

set fire to rose princess blankets.

disrupting the calm of a quiet home

and spilling the innocent blood of

dear Aiyana.

seven.

dear Aiyana,

seven.

dear Aiyana,

seven-years-old.

second grade,

single digit number,

a baby learning the world

and the cruelties that come hidden within it.

gentle child of God

robbed of her life,

victim of a police brutality state,

victim of a heinous system riddled with lies and deception,

do you hear her name?

do you see her face in every young black girl?

the cries of Aiyana and family

should shake the nation to its core.

beautiful girl, your cries are heard.

you have been silenced by the media, silenced by the blue,

silenced by your country.

this world will not find peace

until you do.

i'll give you the megaphone to scream your story.

i'll give you the stage to stand on.

i'll give you my shoulder to lean on.

dear girl,

in Heaven, i pray you are a princess

with a dazzling crown on your head with rubies.

may you roam the golden streets and grin.

may your heart be filled with delight and may

fear never pierce your heart again.

may your stride be bouncy and wild with skipping

and hopscotch.

may your only choices be between

playing jacks or playing hide and seek.

Aiyana Monet Stanley-Jones,

your life mattered.

your life will continue to matter.

your life will extend beyond the confines

of a mortal body.

may you rest softly

as we fight for your justice.

July 20, 2002 – May 16, 2010

hot coffee

you are the sunrise.

hot coffee in the very first break of morning,

sipped cautiously over daydreams of

future and past.

you are the sunset.

hot tea in the very eve of the day,

filled with flowers and herbs

from the garden that we planted ourselves.

don't forget me

when the sun goes away.

forgotten dreams

the moon has risen, yet i won't sleep,

[don't have me drift into slumber].

i want to spend the next millennium holding you tightly,

[and listening to the sound of your melodic breathing].

your heartbeat is like a drum,

keeping me awake and reminding me that the man i love

is only a few thump-thump-thumps away.

[it terrifies me that the beating can be stolen

by a man in blue with a gun].

i stare at the stars and i whisper a prayer.

tangled in blankets together,

i thank god that you are still in my arms.

[held there by love and faith alone].

my heart beating in three-fourths time,

[i can feel the anxious skipping]

15

missing [and craving]

the softness [and gentleness]

of your lips.

i veil my face from the light of day

to keep my eyes fixed the dream of you and i.

that's only place i can touch your face

without the fear of what may happen next.

[i write a lot about love for someone

who knows nothing about it.]

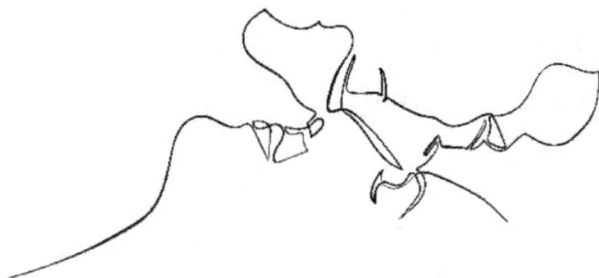

paint

i see you the way Van Gogh saw yellow.
it's consuming, vibrant, and everywhere.
the hues sink deeply into
every chair,
every hill,
every mountain.

the intensity and fervor
bleeding into the paintbrush
and into skin.
a budding addiction, an artistic obsession,
a yearning for warmth.

and that's the way
the cookie crumbles

when i saw you kicking the bottom

of the vending machine on the third floor

of the english building,

i knew i was going to fall in love with you.

with every

"give!
me!
my!
pinwheels!"

my heart pounded through my chest

and threatened to come up through my throat.

and it could be because i find the mere prospect

of someone so desperate for a chocolate cookie

that they'll resort to violence intriguing,

or maybe it's because of the way you doodle

in your notebook during the lectures in mr. o'neil's class.

perhaps it's how you smirk at me
when i'm the first one to raise my hand
to answer a question about british literature.

or maybe it's none of that.
maybe with every swift kick to the machine,
you remind me of everything i am not.

you are a police siren blaring at two in the morning
and i am the unlucky bystander next to the
convenient store that just got robbed.

you are what it feels like to run barefoot down
an empty castle and sing at the top of your lungs
because the acoustics are *perfect,* and you aren't afraid
to take up space in this world.

you are a tiger that just learned how to open its cage
and i am the fresh-faced zookeeper, first day on the job.
we both are co-existing with each other
and we're both at odds at the same time.
we are oil and water,

two positive magnets,

the sun and the moon.

and still, here you are,

kicking a vending machine.

and i am so in love with you.

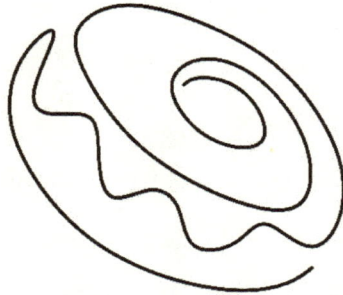

love loudly

i sip from an overflowing cup, similar

to how an animal would, except

my drink is scalding my lips and

tearing the back of my throat into blisters, but i can't stop.

that's what loving you is like.

i'm sorry my love is so messy and loud,

it's filled with sobs and long nights with the overwhelming

urge to grab onto you and never let go.

but i swear to you,

i don't know how to love any other way.

21

constellations

you deserve the universe
on a silver platter,
yet, here i am, a single star,
a dot in the galaxy of
what you warrant.

i'm so lucky to be a part
of your solar system.

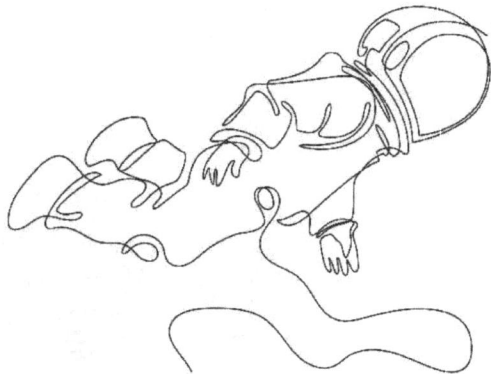

if i could speak
to Elijah McClain...

gentle soul made of dance moves

and twirls around the house,

gentle soul made of snapping fingers,

jazz squares, dance parties, a grin a mile wide

and soft moves made onto a violin,

you did everything right. you did everything right.

boy of no more than twenty-three

was stolen by the boys in blue,

was taunted by the boys in blue,

was killed by the boys in blue,

will be memorialized by the people in black.

gentle soul of no more than twenty-three

wore his heart on his sleeve

just in case someone needed a piece of it.

gentle soul whose bones were

made of music

and love,

whose hands were softly stitched and

shaped perfectly to hold his bow.

gentle boy,

you did

everything

right

and you were still taken away

from the world in the cruelest of manners.

you deserve the symphonies

that you put out into the world.

you deserve

greater than any standing ovation.

rest how you lived,

gently.

February 25, 1996- August 24, 2019

wild

loving you is like being caught
in the eye of a storm.
quiet and hesitant, yet,
surrounded by a fierceness so
wild and rare that it can
shake trees, tear apart the ground,
change the environment so
severely it's unrecognizable.
it can push away anything that
tries to stop it.

our love is so passionate and
dangerous that no man would
dare try to pull us apart.
you are the wind and i am the rain,
you are the lightening and i am the thunder,
our love is strong enough
to be a hurricane.

25

let me get lost in you.

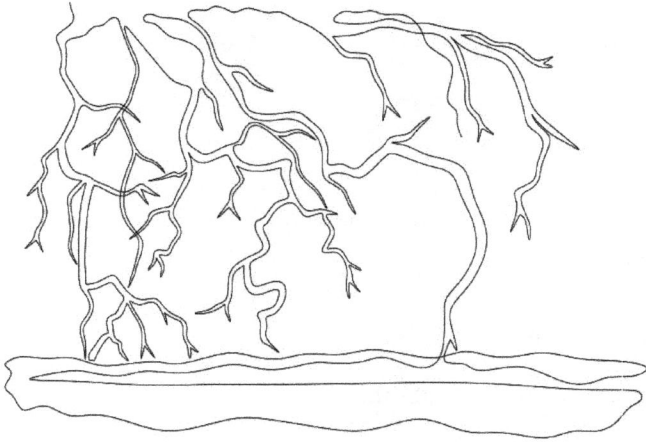

nirvana

compared to you

and all of your beauty,

Heaven is just a name

and a place in the sky.

the sky and her gods

i knew you were the one

when you said you loved my poetry

the way that you loved the night sky.

with a glimmering admiration that

would make Greek gods green with envy

and blue with longing.

brown girls

brown skinned girl,

lips flushed with color and eyes deep as the Nile,

hidden under bushels of midnight curls,

shields her eyes under rose colored frames;

head bobbing to j.cole, foot tapping to Michael,

soul searching for Aretha, heart yearning for Tupac;

brown skinned girl,

tracing patterns through torn jeans,

tying up bantu knots and painting statues of settlers with

cocoa butter,

speaking to the gods with every finna, gunna, holla,

fluent in ebonics, fluent in the sound of harlem; new orleans;

memphis;

braiding hair to scalp and to soul,

wrapping up her work in silk headscarves;

brown skinned girl,

raised in the church, raised in the home, raised in the

streets,

family matters and saturday cookouts,
watching auntie make the potato salad, falling in dance lines and
falling in love;

brown skinned girl,
melanin mixed with gold, glowing;
tongue like a bullet with the words she speaks,

wide eyes,
fierce as fire,
swift as the rivers,
strong as the earth.

7 deadly sins

the day you first kissed me

was the day i realized

exactly why lust was a deadly sin.

(and i made sure to

embrace myself as a sinner).

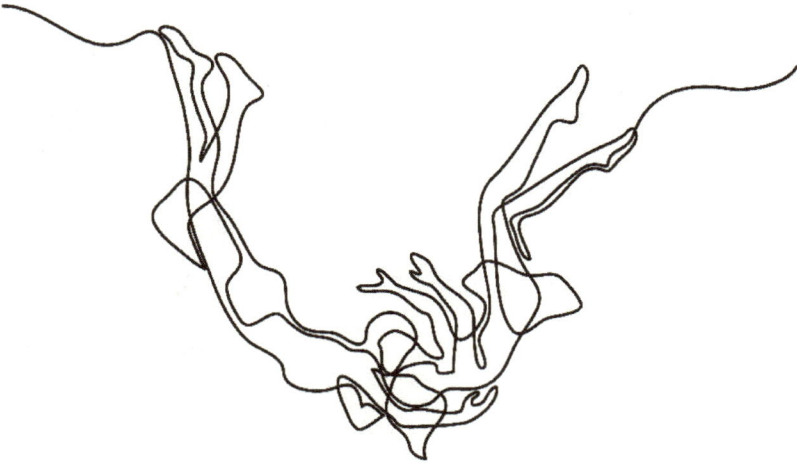

passion

i saw your vulnerability hiding
between perfumed sheets.
your love was like an inferno,
breathtaking, passionate, scalding,
my sideways heart spilled out
with warmth burning every inch of me.

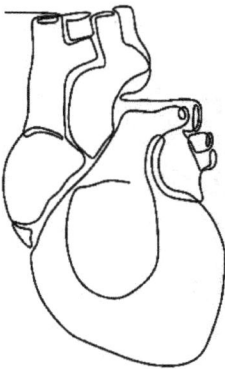

your intimacy touched
giving the pieces of myself i never
cared to deal with.
your love is like a spanish lullaby,
fire in every flicker,
and i've never been warmer.

intimacy

falling asleep with you is like

falling in love all over again.

the butterflies burrow in my stomach and

my heart beats faster than the wings

of the hummingbird,

yet manages to stay in time with

every rise and fall of your chest.

if i could bottle up moments

and save them i would,

but moments were meant to be moments

and not much more.

flowers

bruised knuckles and brown paper skin

are all that is left of me as i write the words

that i hope will soothe your mind.

here i am, pink and starry-eyed,

dying to hear your voice and

watch the color sprout from your chest.

i can feel your bated breath

lingering on my neck,

but when i reach in vain and greed,

i get burned by our passion.

i realize that some things are

too precious to be touched.

let me write *fragile* on your arms.

i bet your lips taste like poetry and

your tongue, religion.

they both have the power to bring men to

their knees in awe,

oh, sobbing awe.

i can hear your heartbeat in iambic pentameter and

now i know why they say that

life imitates art, art imitates life,

and you are a masterpiece.

my dear, you've planted seeds in my lungs,

and because they are beautiful

i simply have refused to cut the

blossoming violets.

if i die by your hand i will have died a hero's death.

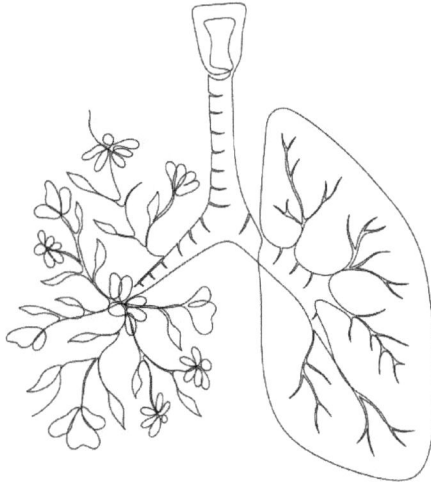

stuck

you are what poems are made of.

raw, unfiltered love,

rays of sunshine and happiness,

the kind of love that sticks like honey

and shines like morning dew.

adventures atop mountains

the hills pulled us in with their stories of rolling thunder
and "hush, baby" lullabies.
i am wrapped up in the arms of the mountains,
bathed in soft moonlight and freshly fallen snow.

i found myself falling for you like an avalanche,
quickly and with absolutely no time to run or hide.
before you cracked open our book
i had no idea that i could become a bystander
in my own novel.

in the january woods i wove my soul back together
with leaves and snowflakes,
each one different than the last,
each one rebuilding the fibers that had been
ripped apart or melted away.

to be without you is the stiffest cold.

it's to be encased in a never-ending permafrost,

to meet jack frost while he is in mourning.

you're the shelter i find when the blizzard is raging.

you are "home" in every sense of the word,

you are the first few steps inside a warm house and

i am a lowly hiker,

ready to go inside after a long day.

you are my solace in this ice age

and my candlelight when the sky turns to black

and invites the stars to come out and play.

cozy

if you listen to the sound of birds chirping

at six in the morning, right when the sun

cracks the sky and

orange and yellow hues paint the horizon—

if you snuggle under a blanket in the middle

of snowy january—

if you feel the beat from the sound of your

favorite song on a quiet day,

you'll know how it feels to love you.

from the other perspective
(across the room)

the neon lights make it hard to see your eyes.

they're deep as the mariana trench

and just as dangerous, i'd bet.

                    the music is pounding through the atmosphere

                        and ripping apart any semblance of peace

                                    or silence.

                    there's no getting away from that look in your eyes.

i've wanted to be yours since before i knew you.

i've walked the earth barefooted and alone

with only a canteen of water

and a dollar to my name,

but with you i'm wine drunk and money pours

from every pocket i have.

                        the smoke has reached the ceiling

                    and i am holding all my secrets in my hands

and hiding them behind my back.
how about we play "spin the bottle", baby?
i'll be your bedsheets if you let me.
i'll wrap you up in so much devotion
you'll never praise anything else again.

i don't know you,
i don't need to.
there's no sins between strangers
and no secrets between friends.
i'll snatch that cigarette from your mouth
and crush it between the folds in this
old couch,
here's an excuse to go outside.
got a light?

i'll kiss the ring on your finger
if you promise to take it off for tonight.
i'll hold you close in my arms
if you promise to throw your phone away.

what your man doesn't know

won't kill him.

floodwater

once upon time, there was
a girl whose life was the text found
in fairy tales.

whose perception of the world was built upon
the blue radiance of a television screen.
love was a concept too
impossible to be real,
too fictional to coexist with a very real body.

yet, i found comfort in the hum of a screen,
its whimsy and light filling my mind with the idea
that i could one day be loved the way
the prince loves the princess.

life is funny that way,
giving false hope to the hopeful
and breaking the spirits of the young.

every time i'd reach out for love

my fingertips would graze the glass

and i'd pray to any god listening

to grace me with the feeling of being wanted.

i prayed on each word like a sinner does

when faced with his last day.

i prayed like the wind and the moon and the stars

had all vanished.

i prayed like i was a doe lost from her mother,

searching from field to empty field

for proof that i wasn't alone.

and yet, nothing came.

it seems that God only knows how to

communicate

through an endless silence.

ten thousand evenings later,

i stumbled into bed and wrapped myself up

under the sheets.

i ignored all the warning signs and put on

rose colored glasses to ignore the red flags

that hung like nooses from the ceiling.

the darkness bled into the morning.

my world was flooded with the waters of the

red sea,

and my ovaries sprouted tumors.

this is where the story begins.

this is where god takes his unannounced departure and i

am stolen away by silver screens and

film directors with venom in between their teeth.

and i, the floss, used and discard after an oscar, because

everyone loves the sick girl and her story always sells.

everyone loves the sick girl who is too fragile to hold

a lit candlestick to,

whose life is written and directed by mr. ovarian tumor.

tossed around like bad plot lines,

"black girl fights for her life" is too tragic,

"unexpected cancer takes over" is too graphic,

but everyone loves a "based on a true story".

this is the rising action,

this is when prayers go unanswered, when

determination turns to desperation,

when my life is circling around in the hands of God

and no one is getting dizzy except for me,

when my lifeblood turns into carboplatin, taxol,

cyclobenzaprine,

the doctors keep taking out the pieces that are corrupted

while im desperately clawing my way

through the operating doors.

am i going to touch the face of God

before my parents do?

this is the climax,

this is the ins and outs of hospital rooms,

prescriptions wringing my neck like a serpent,

the somber talks with oncologists,

telling me about my options,

what options?

hebrews eleven: one reads,

"now faith is the assurance of things hoped for,

the conviction of things not seen".

this is the part of the film where

sweet boy meets sick girl.

when fragile bones are held

and kept warm.

hospitals are now city banks,

and we're Bonnie and Clyde.

facing death is less scary

when you're not facing it alone.

and when God

sent Noah the dove,

he didn't shy away.

so what kind of fool would i be

to ignore a sign of peace?

with my body broken,

he takes my hand,

and he calls me beautiful

when i'm dripping in disease.

he isn't afraid to kiss my head

where my hair has faded.

the love that we show

emits pure gospel,

so loud that the sound

falls upon the ears of my God and

he apologizes for the flood.

it seems that God only knows how to

communicate

through an endless silence.

eyes

the first time i saw you
i noticed the stars in your eyes.
in the black of night, the
constellations hid themselves under
the darkened chestnut
and made it hard to see their shine.

but in the sun, oh man,
the stars shine so brightly and
reflect the color of sweet praline.
you've given me a sweet tooth.

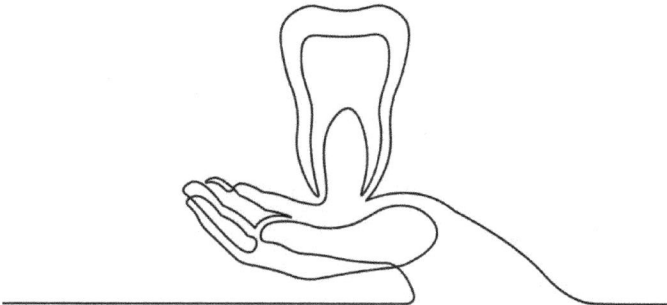

fortune is in your touch

with all the gifts i've been given,

all the blessings i've received,

i never imagined i'd be so fortunate

to hold something as precious

as your hand.

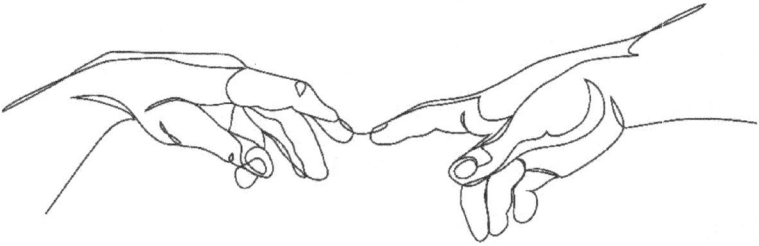

what to do when the love is gone

i hope one day you drown in the sorrows

you forced me to wade through.

i hope the love that we shared turns to

thick lava and flows through your veins,

bubbling and popping as it tries to escape.

i hope the other woman bursts into hives

and rashes,

i hope her tongue curdles and her hair thins.

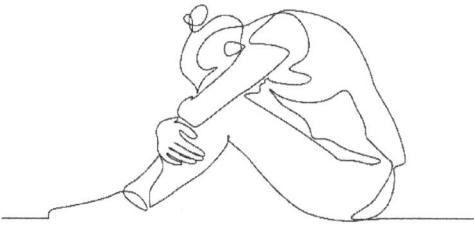

but most of all,

i hope that one day

i love myself enough

to recover from your infidelity.

serpents and apples

is man sinful due to the actions of eve,
or the inactions of adam?

is the first bite
any more guilty than the second?

is the serpent the villain
or the hero?

and while we're asking impossible questions,
how long does it take
to heal a broken heart?

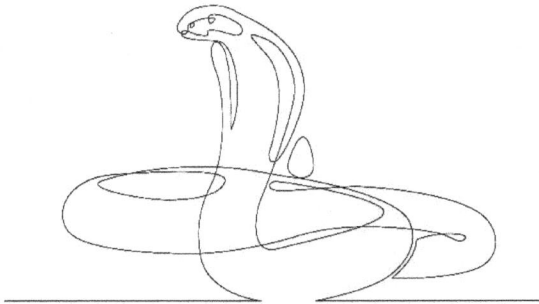

fire starter

my bones are made of

gunpowder and rope.

i go through life as a ticking time bomb

of my own creation.

what a shame it is

that i shared a bed with a match

and gasoline.

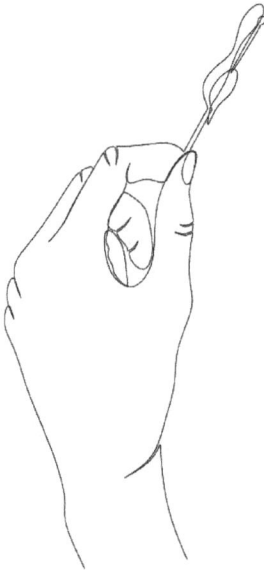

read the map

my poetry is a literary map,

allowing me to see behind corners and over walls in places

i could only dare to dream of.

the words guide me to a lost girl,

not yet a woman, yet no longer cloaked by innocence.

her skin is made of glass, proudly showing her

reds, blues, and purples.

all bumping and beating in the same rhythm

in a dire panic.

it's hard to keep yourself warm

when your bones are frozen solid.

the lines underneath her eyes

and sagging cheekbones tell a story that reads,

"the passage of time has not been kind".

the veins from her neck down

are filled with gasoline

and each painful pump

of her matchbox heart is a warning.

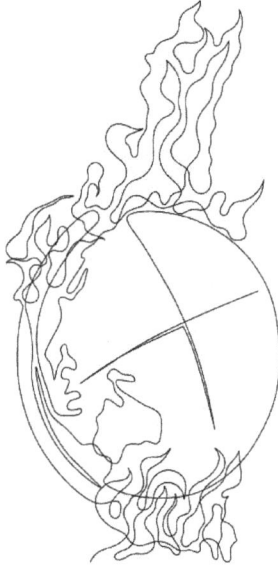

she'll light the world around her on fire.

ring-ring

listening to the hum of the telephone

as i wait for you to answer

is like listening to a death march.

the "*your call has been forwarded—*"

is a brutal reminder that i am

replaceable at best.

i know your number by heart

but i know you don't know mine.

i guess i'll try calling again.

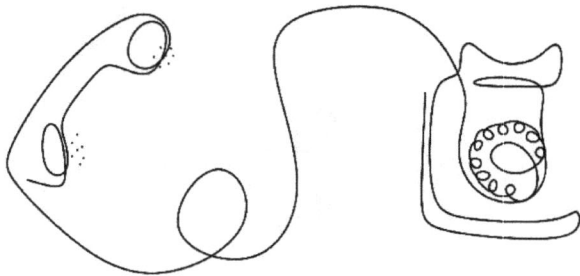

love is to be given and taken away

they say—
"we accept the love
we think we deserve".

if that's true,
then why do i dig through boxes of old photographs
and cry over the way your eyes gleam?

what compels my breaking heart
to further shatter
by holding your sweatshirt to my chest
and apologizing for an act i did not commit?

why do i find myself enraptured by you
after you painted the stars in my sky
but gifted her the whole universe?

i believe we accept the love

we wish we had.

enough

is it inherently poetic to be tricked by love?
is it poetic to be a victim to love,
a devotee to the concept of love,
a lemming to the mere thought?

is it poetic to fall into the delusions of handsome devils,
to forgive, and to forgive, and to forgive?
to pick apart your body for each slash
and apologize to the butcher?

is it poetic to wonder why your brown skin
wasn't enough?
why your silly jokes,
your singing, though off-key,
your touch,
wasn't enough for the man
who claimed to be driven by love?

when your "enough" is tossed onto the cutting board

and chopped up into

fine bits of self-doubt and self-loathing,

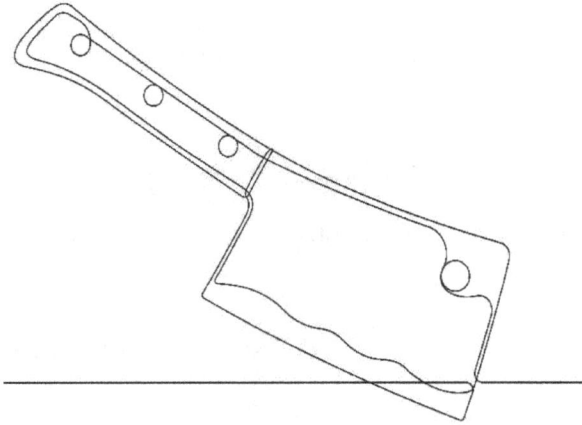

is it possible to ever truly be enough?

pills, baby

your love is a drug.

take one in the morning,
with a kiss on the neck and a
smile.

repeat every chance you get
refills on this prescription: ∞

(i never stopped to think—
am i addicted?)

bedsheets

my skin crawls with envy when i think of your bedsheets,

how they comfort you through the

cold of the night, the raging of storm,

the shining of sun.

if i could hold you half as gently

i'd never let go.

how unfair the world is

that something so lifeless and thin gets

to hold you in a way i cannot.

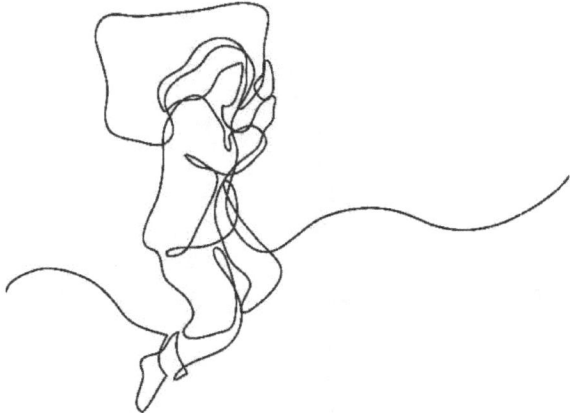

jealousy is a compliment

you light up a room so well

that you make the sun and stars

sick with envy.

keep shining, handsome boy.

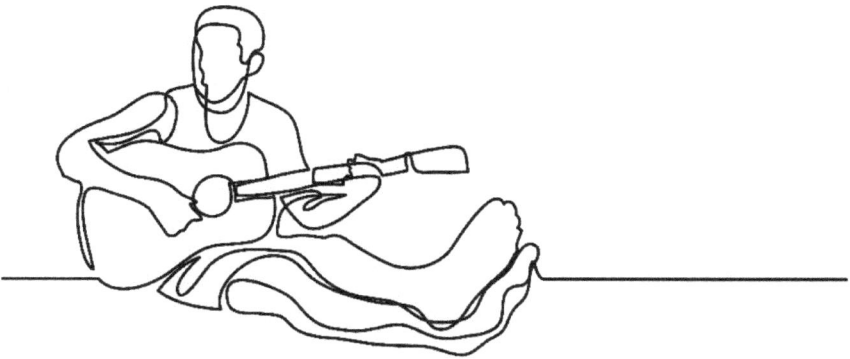

spanish sundays

kiss me while i'm in delusion and then

maybe we can both feel something real.

put your lips on the depressed girl

and then maybe you can say you've done something poetic.

the girl who sees her phantoms in every shade of white,

who walks down the road at night

waiting for the city to suck the sorrows from her chest

and turn it into something extraordinary.

the girl who is too much,

the girl whose heart is spilling over with milk and honey and

who can only speak in riddles.

the girl who wants to touch the palm of your hand with hers

and remind you why you are beautiful.

the girl who wants to love but
is too afraid to lose love, who
prides herself on being a conundrum.
who's a manic pixie dream girl in
broken down sneakers and baseball caps,
whose hands shake at the faintest semblance of hesitance,
that girl will love warm.

that girl gives quiet nights wrapped in stardust and
morning haikus about how nicely your hand feels in hers.
she'll sing loudly and unapologetically.
she'll think in musical notes and villanelles.

the girl will underline and highlight
in every book she owns because
she wants to make every sure every beautiful thought
can pull you in and caress you when she can't.

her love is fire on a day with no sun.

the words we don't say aloud

tell me you can still hear my voice

when i speak to you.

tell me that you still feel my touch

even after we've parted.

tell me that i am what you want,

even if you don't mean it.

breathe my name in like it's all that you've ever craved,

delete her photos from your phone.

you shaped music notes like clay with her.

her melodic voice rattled through the confines of your room

like a terrible secret, and

i bet you bragged to your friends about it.

i know they still ask about her music.

do they ask about my poetry?

tell me,

why does she still call you?

(and why do you still call her?)

punishment

if i could make you crawl through the dirt

on your belly like a serpent,

if i could have you trek through the depths of hell

with water dangled right before your eyes,

if i could have you drain the ocean

one drop at a time,

i wouldn't.

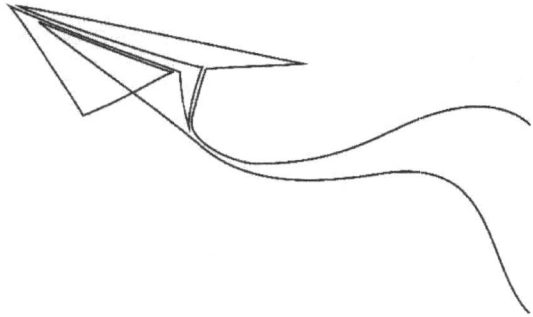

i'd ask for the love you gave

to return to sender.

black boy, joy

black boy,

do you love yourself?

did you watch the sky last night, black boy?

the universe called you by name.

she said,

"*black* boy, gifted with my color,

gifted with my power,

gifted with my vastness,

do you love yourself?"

black boy,

do you love yourself?

do you love the melanin in your skin, your eyes,

deep as the rivers flowing through the heart of Africa?

do you love *your* Africa?

do you yearn for the place that bore you?

black boy,

do you love the stars God put in your eyes?

do you love the voice He gave you?

a gift of silver lungs and a tone that booms of rolling

thunder,

do you revel in your glory, black boy?

black boy,

do you love yourself?

do you love the gentleness that you have been granted?

your heart as soft as the waves

you brush through your hair.

do you love the curls that sprout from your scalp?

each tightly woven, each with a story?

black boy,

do you love yourself?

your existence is a love poem from God.

your smile is a signed contract with the world that reads,

"i am black boy joy."

"i am black boy excellence."

"i am."

70

black boy,

love yourself as the universe loves you.

                                        unconditionally.

loving (1967)

yes,

beautiful man of cold skin,

you are shades darker than the gentle black of my own.

but please, hold my hand,

carry my body through the sea of onlookers

who spit "infidel" and "heretic" in our faces.

i'll take your name,

Loving,

i'll wrap my lips around those two syllables

and kiss it before bed every night.

i'll hold you tightly

and rock you to sleep,

even when the bricks shatter our kitchen window.

i'll marry you in D.C.,

i'll marry you in Virginia,

i'll marry you on the bloodied steps of the

highest court in the land,

i'll marry you in ten thousand different lifetimes.

Dedicated to Richard and Mildred Loving, pioneers for the legalization
of interracial marriage. Keep on loving.

he used to call me "hummingbird".

little hummingbird,

with feathers ruffled,

small eyes,

small heart.

pulled from the scribes of old papyrus,

life was whispered into you by Amun,

god of the sun and the air.

kissed by the gods and in your creation,

you were gifted with love.

your wings are small,

yet powerful,

slashing through the air with a gracefulness that would

threaten even the most well-trained ballerina.

faster than a flowing river,

smoother than silk,

doused in sugar and

hand painted by the angels.

little hummingbird,

i see the way you linger

outside of his apartment window.

i see the eagerness in your sway,

in the morse code

you tap onto the glass window every morning.

i see the yearning in your eyes.

i see you begging for the lock

at the bottom of the glass to

click

and release,

so that you may,

(once again),

have a chance to turn a house

into a home.

but his love for you has reached its expiration date.

little hummingbird,

i can smell your desperation,

it's sticking to your wings
like tar and is dragging you down.

i know you think he's the answer.
you think that his touch
is the air you breathe.

but if he loved you
the way you love the sky,
he would have pulled the earth up with his hands
and made his nest with you.

the things we stole
from the future

every time i dream of you it turns out to be a nightmare.

your love has been tainted in my mind

and now all i can do is pretend you aren't

lurking through the shadows in the corners of my room.

i wear a silk scarf around my eyes

and stuff my mouth with clay

whenever i know you're near

because it's easier to pretend you're not there

than to speak your name

or to see the eyes of a betrayer.

you used to tell me we'd take the whole world.

we'd stuff artifacts in our pockets,

we'd drain the seven seas and bottle them in

pretty jars and label them

"the things we stole from the future".

we'd go on an epic journey together,

we'd fill the hearts of strangers with our moving tales

of heroism and young love.

we'd tear apart the threads of the universe

and sew them into tacky sweaters and scarves.

we'd make art out of everything we got our hands on,

we'd toss our fears into the fire,

we'd mold out names into the earth,

we'd write our love into the clouds.

i've scrubbed every inch of my body raw

trying to get rid of the lingering remnants of your touch.

but when i explore the suds that drip down my legs

all i can do is see the places

you touched her instead of me.

was her touch just as soft?

was her kiss just as gentle?

i hope if the regret boils you alive on summer nights

and freezes you to your core in winter.

i hope if the pet names you called her

left sores on your tongue and in your throat.

i hope the world sees you for what you are
and what you have done.
i hope karma kisses you passionately
and without a second thought.

my love for you was invitation only
and you allowed her to crash the party.
it's a roller coaster ride that's had more downs
than ups and i so desperately just
wanted to get off.

and as i flip through my scriptures to
recover from the trauma you gave me,
i felt the shiver of a prayer run down my spine
and just as i whispered your name to God,
you screamed mine to Lucifer.

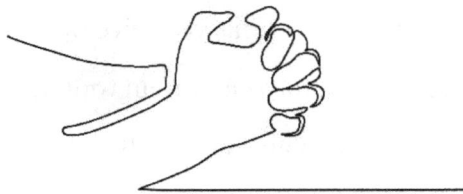

forgiveness

a haiku

enraptured by you,

the severity of sin

no longer matters.

escaping from eden

big man,

lean as a redwood tree and with skin

the color of deep earth.

keep walking.

if we make the slightest gaze back

we'll surely turned to dust.

he whispers the gospel under his breath

and lets his tongue hang on to every word

the way he holds onto a lover.

big man,

do the lines on the palms of your hand form a map?

do they tell you where i have been and where i am going

when your fingers interlock with mine?

do you feel my heartbeat

through the roots that run underground

and connect with your veins?

big man,

hold me softly. hold me right.

i am awful for you and you are awful for me,

but we are perfect in every disturbed moment.

when the sun sets in the west

and the sky turns purple and orange,

will you protect me from the spirits that

roam this forest?

will you protect me from the eternal punishments

that await us both?

will you dress me in your tattered robes

when the cold gets to be too much?

will you brush my hair back with your fingers

and count the scars you put on my body?

will you flinch at my touch,

assuming the worst with every sideways glance?

we won't say a word to each other

but we'll speak the languages of the old gods

and relay poetry with skin on skin.

big man,

did you hear what God said?

did you hear the anger in His voice,

how it shook the hills and ruptured the mountains?

have you seen his image in the flowing creek,

in the depths of the caves unexplored?

have you seen him dressed in vine and silk?

have you prayed for him to spare our lives?

or have you only beseeched the Savior

for my benefit?

is your love for me powerful enough

to sacrifice your place in Heaven's court?

do you see Him in the mushroom circles

that hide the fae?

have you whispered nothings to the spirits in the air

and begged them to treat me better

than you ever could?

tell me with your lips the ways in which you intend

to sacrifice yourself.

i've never seen you cry.

could it be that your tears are mixed with the

acid rain that burns our skin whenever

our sins are unearthed?

are you my public penance?

my three hail marys,

my desperate wail to an absent father?

i'll lead you out of the forest with

poison ivy sprouting from the roots in my scalp.

we will braid them together

and face the consequences

as Lilith did with God.

as Cain did with Abel.

as we do

with each other.

forbidden love is always the sweetest

our love is suffering from imposter syndrome.

i'll peer through the cathedral doors and

sneak bread and wine from the church

to feed the beast inside us both.

god have mercy on the young lovers

for they know not what they do.

they link hands and hearts,

they frolic through the forbidden

and love in the boldest of ways.

i'll keep you free from the bloodied jaws

of the sinners that surround us.

i'll encase you in a glass jar

and you'll twirl around like a music box ballerina

to the beating of our hearts

and the shouts of those who call us "heretics".

the world will never know our crystal hearts

or our carbon minds.

take their stares and their scoffs for what they are,

compliments,

and wear them on the cuff of your sleeve.

your poetic nature is a gift

and it will not be hidden.

we are unique to this world of

disastrous love

and we will take claim to our throne of hearts.

so puff out your chest

and hold your tongue,

we're going undercover

and into the world

that wants our love to burn like the fires in Hell.

i'll love you through it all.

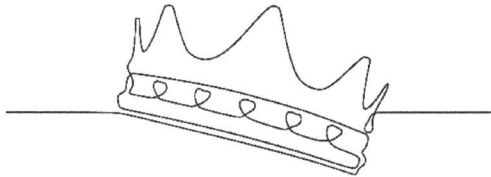

slowly, the seeds will sprout

i'll cautiously rebuild my nest

under the shelter of your ribcage.

i'll kiss the steps leading up to the

front door of our home

and bless the old house with new holy water.

i'll cozy myself up under your

new name, "safety",

i'll keep skin to skin and remind myself

that the past was left in the past for a reason.

i'll hold you tighter than i ever have

and ever will.

i'll sing you melodies about the moon

and the stars.

i'll teach you the way that they dance

and we'll make our living room into a ballroom.

to live cautiously is to waste,

to love cautiously is to thrive.

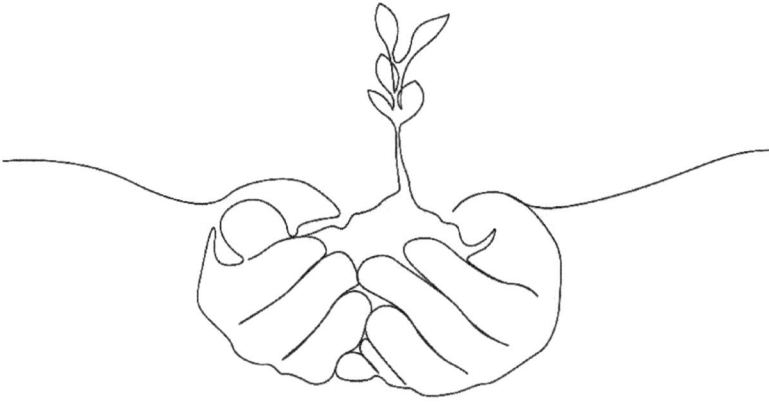

anxiety

i wear rose quartz around my neck

because i hear it is good for love.

i paint my skin with faux gold

because i heard boys like a girl that glows.

[the water is getting higher.]

my insecurities are tucked tightly

under a pile of torn and filthy clothes,

never to be washed.

[the water is getting higher.]

i hid my ugly in packed bags to far off destinations

i never plan on visiting.

i convinced myself that swimming in circles

was the best way to get out of the ocean.

[the water is getting higher.]

i didn't know what calm was like

until you threw me the life preserver

that pulled me out of the riptide.

[the water is getting higher.]

the eye of the storm

you entered my life in the middle of a hurricane.

i set you up a tent and tended to your wounds,

i kissed the bruises on your forehead

and cut the rope from your wrists.

the day i saw you, my heart stopped beating.

instead, she grew legs and she ran,

she ran for the hills and down into the valleys.

love can hard to find, but when you find it,

it'll come home with you like an orphaned pup.

i've seen you in my dreams

and in my nightmares,

i can't decide if that makes you

foreboding or foretold.

but the way you smile at the sky,

the way your laugh sounds like a melody

crafted from instruments that mankind has never seen,

the way you paint pictures with your words

and spread your Midas touch—

i'm willing to take the risk

of adding you to my story book.

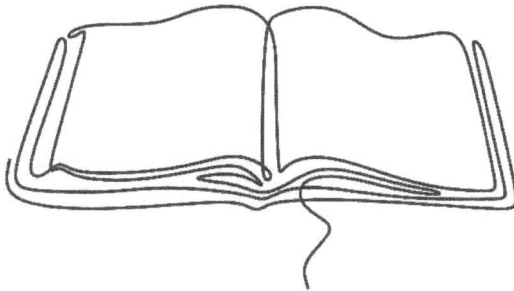

count the seconds

how wonderful and rare it is
to share home, to share bed,
to share laughter and to share love
with a person who feels like a
moment.

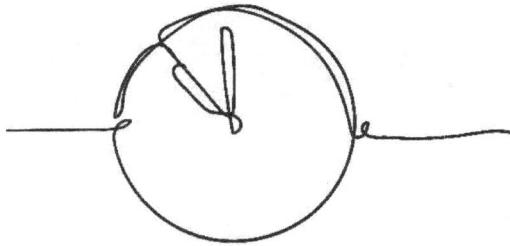

to be drunk and sober

your laughter is a sound so sweet

you must have stolen it from the angels.

your kiss is something so intoxicating

that the fanciest of distilleries cannot replicate

the drunkenness you spark in me.

i'll drink the love you produce

from the dips in your collarbones

and i'll bless every drop of the wine.

the sting of alcohol is nothing

compared to the sharpness of your lips on mine.

the matriarch

dear Gloria,

the sun rises in the east and sets in the west

all to remind you that the day

doesn't ever truly end.

it simply repeats its cycle of

hiding and revealing itself because

it knows that the shine of the sun is incomparable

to the shine of everything that you are.

dear Gloria,

the world spins to the tune of your voice

on a Sunday morning,

your vibrato shaking the walls of the home with

soul and motherly love.

you taught me that my blackness is not

a threat or a curse,

but a blessing from God himself.

that my melanin was crafted by the angels and

that our family will have a legacy because of it.

if i could hold a mirror to you and show you the

solar systems that you have created,

you would gasp at the planets and the moons

and the stars that all have your name.

the good Lord knew what he was doing

when he blessed the earth with you.

dear Gloria,

i hope you know that you are a goddess among

the common woman, an Athena.

a woman who harbors the strength of an ox,

the kindness of a newborn doe

and the fierceness of the wind.

the way you show the world just who you are

through the power of your voice

and the firmness of your stance

proves that fire can be warm and comforting

as well as scalding and brave.

you have walked ten thousand miles
while carrying the earth on your shoulders.
you have faced the lightning and the thunder
and reminded the sky that you don't back down
under the pressure of rain.
you do not bow down to the threats of the earth.

my dear grandmother,
to begin to thank you is to cross the ocean alone.
it is to find my way back home through the twists of a forest,
it is to count a million reasons on my fingers
and start all over again once i hit the last digit.

to describe the depths of your power
and the vastness of your spirit is to
ask God himself how he created a woman who
shaped the world of others with her bare hands.
the woman who carved the pieces that built me and
who blessed me with the scriptures she would read,
it is to ask God how he created a being so kind that she
would hold the fragile and the broken in her arms
without asking for anything in return.

it is to ask how

the world was lucky enough

to be blessed by a woman with so much love to give.

Gloria,

you are the love that you give.

black woman, black woman

i am not your little

"chocolate

doll"

i am the earth.

i am the soil in which your food grows.

i am the ground in which your babies play on.

i am the wind and the sky and the moon above.

listen,

do you hear the crashing of the waves?

do you taste the salt on your tongue?

do you feel the sand on your feet?

i am black as the midnight sea

during high tide.

i don't "talk too loud"

my voices ricochets off the walls that you

sealed around the women that

dared to call you out.

the curls that fall down the sides of my face

remind me of all the curves that come with this

black body,

all the knots and styles and culture

that are deeply rooted in this skin.

i am a masterpiece, not a side piece,

i am the super to your nova,

and i will be treated with respect.

i have sewed lines into every open stitch on this earth.

i have flooded the cosmos with my melanin.

i have built my armor in ten thousand shades of black.

i have secured my chest plate and strapped on my shield,

i have walked through the valley of the shadow of death

and made it to the end

and i've seen the light.

and baby,

that light shone so *good*

on my black skin.

a page from Poseidon's diary

i remember the way the sky looked when
you pulled me outside of the apartment
in the middle of the night.

you said,
"our love is like the ocean, baby.
unexplored and dangerous."

you said,
"one of these days, baby,
i'm taking us to the beach.
i want you to look across the ocean skyline
and predict our future in the waves."

i remember the way the ground felt
when our earthquake steps sunk
into the ground.
you rose castles out of the sand

and made the hermit crabs your serfs.

you said,

"baby, look at our kingdom come.

our arms are wide enough for the world."

i let you lead me to the water with

a naïve grandeur.

you pulled the blue from the sky

and had it wrapped around our lungs like silk.

we breathed in air and out bubbles

and forgot the meaning of the word "drown".

we lived under seashells and played games with blue tangs.

you hid your sorrows in shipwrecks

and left them for the ghosts of the past.

we descended into the dark

and replaced the stars with starfish.

we made our home in the coral reefs and

disguised ourselves as sharks

to protect the guppies.

we were shielded in our own world.

we locked hands

and i swear,

the way your fingers connect with mine is the closest

mankind will ever get to proving that

magic is real.

i found our love in underwater caves,

scratched along the sides in a language long forgotten.

i found our love in every grain of sand,

in every pebble,

in every blade of sea grass.

i found our love in the ocean,

above the waves,

and everywhere in between.

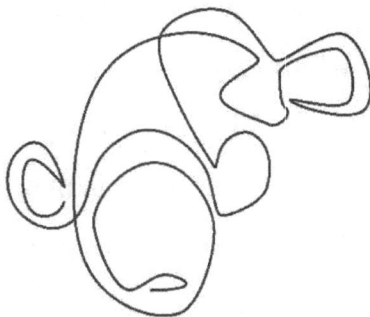

an excerpt from the new aged Bible

love is colored black.

it is deep and undeniably rich,

a spiritual renaissance like no other.

press your palms against mine

and we'll take on the world together

one step at a time.

i'll read you like the scriptures

and lift you higher than the tallest mountains.

i'll keep you safe from those

who wish to pull you down

and cover you in their sheets of hatred.

love is colored black

and you are the most incredible shade of
midnight.

may i one day be lucky enough

to scatter the stars through your atmosphere.

to love while black is to riot

i have seen his face in every black man.
i felt the drip of blood that
rolled down his cheek like the many
before him.

"i can't breathe!"
"mama! mama!"

i've clenched my fists together and dug my nails
into the palms of my hands,
i've prayed harder than a sinner on death row,
i've begged the Lord to show mercy.

i've held my heart in my hands
and comforted it better than anyone else could ever try to.
i've carried this bag of collective pain over my shoulder
and dragged it across the Sahara,
through the thick and unforgiving clouds of

injustice that cut like specks of sand during a
windstorm.

i've pushed my way through the morgue while
holding a Bible to my chest,
i've cried with them all and loved with them all.

my blackness could get me killed and yet i revel in it.
i dance in my brown skin, i kiss in my brown skin,
i love in my brown skin.
my brown skin is the beginning and the end,
my brown skin is Holy and worthy of being praised,
my brown skin is the closest thing God ever got
to making something perfect.

my outspokenness is a sin amongst myself.
i prance up and down the street screaming my gospel
and don't care who calls me "aggressive".
you haven't seen aggressive.

i refuse to be a part of the
selective memory society.

i will acknowledge my blackness with pride
and with valor.
i will speak the names of the murdered unapologetically
and make the atmosphere tense.
i will relish in the discomfort and remind myself that
those who came before me knew pain worse than i do.

to love while black is to riot.
to hold hands and walk down streets
splattered with the blood of the innocent
and the young and be labeled as
"thugs" while demanding justice be served
is to riot.

to keep an open mouth and an open mind
in times where the man in the oval office
is prioritizing silence
is to riot.

to hold onto hope when all hope is lost is to riot.
to show vulnerability when the world is against you
and against all who look like you

is the most politically incorrect thing

a black person can do.

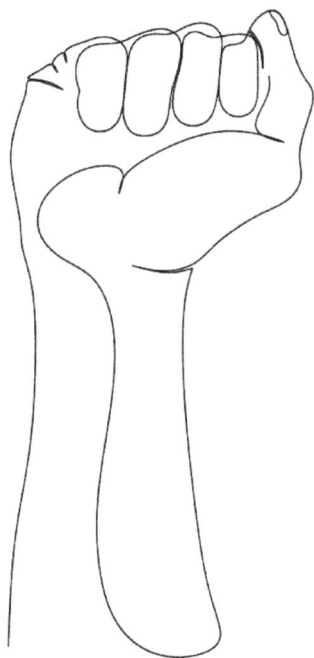

in memoriam.

Tamir Rice (12yrs),

Emmett Till (14yrs),

Breonna Taylor (26yrs),

Trayvon Martin (17yrs),

Elijah McClain (23yrs),

Aiyana Stanley Jones (7yrs),

George Floyd (46yrs),

Tommie McGlothen Jr. (44yrs),

Wavey Austin (63yrs),

Atatiana Jefferson (28yrs),

Trayford Pellerin (31yrs),

Aura Rosser (40yrs),

Stephon Clark (22yrs),

Tyre King (13yrs),

Willie McCoy (20yrs),

Javier Ambler (40yrs),

Botham Jean (26yrs),

Philando Castille (32yrs),

Alton Sterling (37yrs),

Andre Green (15yrs),

Michael Brown (18yrs),

Tanisha Anderson (37yrs),

Eric Garner (43yrs),

Oscar Grant (22yrs),

Sean Bell (23yrs),

Gabriella Nevarez (22yrs),

Akai Gurley (28yrs),

Walter Scott (50yrs),

LaQuan McDonald (17yrs),

Freddie Gray (25yrs),

Kathryn Johnston (92yrs),

Korryn Gaines (23yrs),

Tanisha Anderson (37yrs),

Michelle Cusseaux (50yrs),

Charleena Lyles (30yrs),

Pearlie Golden (93yrs),

Kayla Moore (41yrs),

India Kager (27yrs),

Sandra Bland (28yrs),

Ahmaud Arbery (25yrs),

Sean Reed (21yrs),

Steven Taylor (33yrs),

Ariane McCree (28yrs),

Terrence Franklin (22yrs),

Miles Hall (23yrs),

Samuel David Mallard (19yrs),

Kwame "KK" Jones (17yrs),

De'Von Bailey (19yrs),

Christopher Whitfield (31yrs),

Eleanor Bumpurs (66yrs),

Tyisha Miller (19yrs),

Natasha McKenna (37yrs),

Bettie Jones (55yrs),

Quintonio LeGrier (19yrs),

Sean Monterrosa (22yrs),

Jerame Reid (36yrs),

Jamel Floyd (35yrs),

Dreasjon Reed (21yrs),

Ezell Ford (25yrs),

Manuel "Mannie" Elijah Ellis (33yrs),

Emantic "EJ" Fitzgerald Bradford Jr. (21yrs),

Charles "Chop" Roundtree Jr. (18yrs),

Chinedu Okobi (36yrs),

Antwon Rose Jr. (17yrs),

Henry Dumas (33yrs),

Rita Lloyd (16yrs),

Victor Steen (17yrs),

Alesia Thomas (35yrs),

Chavis Carter (21yrs),

Jamaal Moore Sr. (23yrs),

McKenzie J. Cochran (25yrs),

John Crawford III (22yrs),

Leonard Deadwyler (25yrs),

Ezell Ford (25yrs),

Tanisha N. Anderson (37yrs),

Janisha Fonville (20yrs),

Meagan Hockaday (26yrs),

Mya Shawatza Hall (27yrs),

David McAtee (53yrs),

Saheed Vassell (34yrs),

Stephon Alonzo Clark (22yrs),

Aaron Bailey (48yrs),

Jordan Edwards (15yrs),

Chad Robertson (25yrs),

Alfred Olango (38yrs),

Charleena Chavon Lyles (30yrs),

Charleena Chavon Lyles' unborn child (14-15 weeks).

author's note

The list of names provided in the previous few pages, unfortunately, is far from complete. The suffering that people of color have faced at the hands of police brutality is immeasurable.

As a society we must do better. We must speak up and speak loudly when faced with injustice. To be silent is to be complicit. There is no longer a middle ground.

Get involved. Know who is representing you in your local government. Get familiar with who your district attorney is. Attend protests, attend city council meetings, and get your voice out there. We are stronger together than we are on our own.

To Love While Black Is to Riot is a love letter to the black community, but it is also an open invitation. It is a dream of mine to spark conversation through art.

I wanted to show love in every form it comes in. Love can be dangerous and fun, love can be saddening and heartbreaking, love can be the most painful experience someone can have.

As a black woman, I grew up seeing so much love in my community. Love was- and is- everything. Love can be found in family circles. Love can be two young people going on an adventure together. Love can be smiling at what you see in the mirror. Love can be sour, and love can be sweet.

Love has many faces. It's important that we acknowledge all the manners in which love can emerge and represent itself in this world.

We are facing a paradigm shift in the United States. Following the murder of George Floyd, it became virtually impossible to not acknowledge the blatant and aggressive racism in our society. People marched during a pandemic to bring about change. People of all shades linked together in solidarity and told the world that enough was enough.

We must maintain that same energy. The revolution is not over because time has passed, nor is it over when the media stops reporting the injustice. It will be over when justice is served, and the system is reformed.

It will be an uncomfortable time. It will be scary. It will be dangerous. We must fight for those who can no longer fight for themselves.

To love while black is to riot. It is to fight. It is to create permanent change.

It will take time. It will take effort.
It will take love.

--Regina Williams

✿

"But in the final analysis, a riot is the language of the unheard. And what is it that America has failed to hear? It has failed to hear that the plight of the Negro poor has worsened over the last few years. It has failed to hear that the promises of freedom and justice have not been met."

--Martin Luther King, Jr.

About the Author

Regina Williams is a writer, actress, and activist. "To Love While Black Is to Riot" is her second anthology, following "The Words I Planted in Persephone's Garden". She has an Associate of Arts in Performing Arts and has received multiple awards for her urban and spoken word poetry. She resides in Shreveport, Louisiana with her family and her three cats.

www.ingramcontent.com/pod-product-compliance
Lightning Source LLC
Chambersburg PA
CBHW020550030426
42337CB00013B/1038

* 9 7 8 0 5 7 8 7 7 4 0 1 5 *